perspective, an LLC is a pass-through entity, meaning that business profits and losses are passed through to the owners and reported on their individual tax returns. This structure combines the simplicity of a sole proprietorship with the liability protection of a corporation.

3. S Corporation

I0446445

An S Corporation is a tax designation rather than a business structure. It offers liability protection like a corporation but allows income and losses to pass through to the owners' personal tax returns. This can result in potential tax savings, making it a popular choice for small businesses.

4. C Corporation

A C Corporation is a separate legal entity from its owners, providing the highest level of liability protection. However, it is subject to double taxation, as both the corporation and the shareholders are taxed on profits. While less common for small businesses, C Corporations can be advantageous in certain situations.

Understanding the tax implications of each business structure is crucial for making informed decisions about your business's legal and financial framework.

The choice you make can have significant ramifications on your tax liabilities, personal liability, and overall ease of operation.

Overview of Tax Obligations

Navigating the tax landscape involves understanding the various types of taxes that may apply to your small business. Here's a glimpse into some of the key tax obligations you may encounter:

1. Income Taxes

Income taxes are a core component of small business taxes, and how you report and pay them depends on your business structure. Sole proprietors report business income on their personal tax returns, while other structures, such as LLCs and corporations, have distinct tax filing requirements.

2. Self-Employment Taxes

If you're a sole proprietor or a partner in a partnership, you are subject to self-employment taxes to fund Social Security and Medicare. Understanding how to calculate and pay these taxes is crucial for managing your overall tax liability.

3. Payroll Taxes

Introduction: Understanding Tax Obligations for Small Businesses

Embarking on the entrepreneurial journey is an exhilarating endeavor, marked by the promise of independence and the potential for financial success. However, woven into the fabric of business ownership is the responsibility of navigating the complex world of tax obligations. In this exploration, we will unravel the intricacies of understanding tax obligations for small businesses, shedding light on the significance of taxes, the nuances of different business structures, and the importance of strategic tax preparation.

The Significance of Taxes

Taxes are the lifeblood of any well-functioning society, providing the financial foundation for essential public services, infrastructure development, and government operations. As a small business owner, recognizing the significance of your tax contributions extends beyond mere compliance. Your financial participation fuels the growth and sustenance of the community in which your business operates.

Beyond the civic duty of contributing to the greater good, understanding the impact of taxes on your business is crucial for sound financial management.

Taxes can represent a substantial portion of your business expenses, and navigating the complexities effectively can contribute to the overall success and sustainability of your venture.

Different Business Structures

One of the fundamental considerations when it comes to small business taxes is the choice of business structure. The structure you choose not only influences how you run your business but also determines the tax obligations you'll encounter. Here's a brief exploration of some common business structures:

1. Sole Proprietorship

As a sole proprietor, you and your business are considered one entity for tax purposes. This means that your business income is reported on your personal tax return. While the simplicity of this structure is appealing, it also means that you are personally responsible for any business debts and liabilities.

2. Limited Liability Company (LLC)

An LLC provides a degree of separation between your business and personal liabilities. From a tax

If your business has employees, you'll need to navigate payroll taxes. This includes withholding income and payroll taxes from employee wages and remitting them to the appropriate government agencies. Additionally, as an employer, you have your own payroll tax obligations.

4. Sales Taxes

Sales taxes are imposed on the sale of goods and services and are typically collected by the seller from the customer. However, the rules and rates for sales taxes vary by location, and it's essential to understand and comply with the specific requirements in your business's jurisdiction.

5. Excise Taxes

Certain businesses may be subject to excise taxes, which are often levied on specific goods, services, or activities. For example, businesses involved in the sale of alcohol, tobacco, or transportation services may encounter excise taxes.

6. Property Taxes

If your business owns real property, you may be subject to property taxes levied by local jurisdictions.

Understanding your property tax obligations is essential for budgeting and compliance.

Each type of tax comes with its own set of rules, filing requirements, and potential deductions. Navigating this landscape requires careful attention to detail and a proactive approach to compliance.

Importance of Proper Tax Preparation

Proper tax preparation is not just a matter of compliance; it is a strategic and proactive approach to managing your business's financial health. Here are key reasons why effective tax preparation is crucial:

1. Minimizing Tax Liability

Strategic tax planning allows you to identify opportunities for minimizing your tax liability legally. By understanding the available deductions, credits, and incentives, you can optimize your business's financial position and retain more of your hard-earned income.

2. Avoiding Costly Mistakes

Tax laws are complex and subject to change. Making mistakes in your tax filings can lead to costly penalties and interest. Proper preparation involves staying informed about the latest tax regulations and diligently applying them to your business.

3. Enhancing Financial Planning

A well-thought-out tax strategy is an integral part of your overall financial planning. It enables you to anticipate tax liabilities, plan for major expenditures, and make informed decisions about the financial direction of your business.

4. Contributing to Long-Term Success

Consistent and effective tax preparation is not a one-time activity; it's an ongoing process that contributes to the long-term success of your business. By cultivating a proactive approach to taxes, you position your business for financial stability and growth.

Conclusion

Understanding tax obligations for small businesses is a dynamic and multifaceted undertaking. From choosing the right business structure to navigating various tax types and embracing strategic tax preparation, each step is crucial for your business's financial health and compliance.

As you navigate the intricacies of small business taxes, remember that knowledge is your most powerful tool. Stay informed about changes in tax laws, seek professional advice when needed, and approach tax obligations with a proactive mindset. By doing so, you not only fulfill your responsibilities as a business owner but also set the stage for a prosperous and sustainable entrepreneurial journey.

Tax Deductions for Small Businesses

Navigating the world of small business taxes involves not only understanding your various tax obligations but also leveraging opportunities to minimize your taxable income legally. One powerful tool in your financial arsenal is the strategic use of tax deductions. In this exploration, we will delve into the realm of tax deductions for small businesses, uncovering the potential savings and optimizing your bottom line.

The Significance of Tax Deductions

Tax deductions are expenses that businesses can subtract from their total income, reducing the amount of income subject to taxation. Leveraging deductions effectively can significantly impact your taxable income, ultimately leading to lower tax liabilities. Small business owners are often entitled to a variety of deductions, providing opportunities for both operational and strategic cost savings.

Identifying Deductible Business Expenses

Understanding which expenses qualify as tax-deductible is fundamental to optimizing your tax position. While the specific deductions available to you may vary based on factors such as your business structure and industry, there are common categories of deductible business expenses:

1. Operating Expenses

- **Rent and Lease Payments**: The cost of renting office space or leasing equipment is generally deductible.
- **Utilities**: Expenses related to utilities, such as electricity, water, and internet, are deductible.
- **Office Supplies**: The cost of necessary office supplies, from paper to pens, can be deducted.

2. Business Insurance

- **Premiums**: Payments for business insurance, including liability and property insurance, are deductible.

3. Employee-Related Expenses

- **Salaries and Wages**: The compensation you pay to employees, including bonuses and benefits, is typically deductible.
- **Retirement Plan Contributions**: Contributions to employee retirement plans, such as a 401(k), may be deductible.

4. Travel and Transportation

- **Business Travel Expenses**: Costs associated with business-related travel, including airfare, lodging, and meals, are often deductible.
- **Vehicle Expenses**: If you use a vehicle for business purposes, you may deduct related expenses such as gas, maintenance, and depreciation.

5. Marketing and Advertising

- **Promotional Costs**: Expenses related to advertising and marketing efforts, including digital and traditional methods, are deductible.

6. Professional Services

- **Fees for Professional Services**: Payments made to professionals such as accountants, consultants, and attorneys are generally deductible.
- **Business Software and Subscriptions**: Costs associated with necessary business software and subscriptions may be deductible.

7. Interest Expenses

- **Loan Interest**: Interest paid on business loans or credit cards used for business purposes is often deductible.

8. Depreciation

- **Depreciation of Assets**: The gradual reduction in value of tangible assets, such as equipment or property, can be deducted over time.

9. Home Office Expenses

- **Home Office Deduction**: If you use part of your home exclusively for business, you may be eligible for a home office deduction.

10. Education and Training

- **Work-Related Education**: Expenses related to education and training that directly benefit your business may be deductible.

Maximizing Deductions for Your Small Business

While the list above provides a broad overview, maximizing deductions requires a strategic approach. Here are key tips to help you make the most of available deductions:

1. Keep Detailed Records

Maintaining accurate and detailed records of your business expenses is crucial. This includes receipts, invoices, and other supporting documentation. Cloud-based accounting software can be a valuable tool in this regard.

2. Understand the Specifics of Each Deduction

Different deductions have specific criteria and limitations. Familiarize yourself with the rules governing each deduction to ensure compliance and maximize your savings.

3. Seek Professional Guidance

Tax laws are complex and subject to change. Enlisting the services of a tax professional can provide invaluable guidance, ensuring you don't overlook any eligible deductions and helping you navigate the ever-evolving tax landscape.

4. Consider Section 179 Deduction

Section 179 of the Internal Revenue Code allows businesses to deduct the full purchase price of qualifying equipment and software purchased or financed during the tax year. Understanding and utilizing this provision can lead to significant upfront savings.

5. Explore Tax Credits

While not deductions, tax credits directly reduce your tax liability. Explore available tax credits for small businesses, such as those for research and development or energy-efficient improvements.

6. Regularly Review and Update Your Strategy

As your business evolves, so do your opportunities for deductions. Regularly review your business operations and expenses to identify new opportunities for deductions and ensure ongoing optimization.

Conclusion

Tax deductions are a powerful tool for small businesses, offering opportunities to reduce taxable income and retain more of your earnings. By understanding the range of deductible expenses and implementing a strategic approach to tax planning, you can optimize your business's financial position.

Recordkeeping and Documentation

In the intricate dance of small business management, one of the most crucial partners is meticulous recordkeeping and documentation. Far from being a mere administrative chore, this practice is a linchpin for financial health, regulatory compliance, and strategic decision-making. In this exploration, we will delve into the significance of recordkeeping and documentation for small businesses, examining the benefits, essential elements, and best practices that can set the stage for sustained success.

The Significance of Recordkeeping

Recordkeeping is more than an organizational nicety; it is the cornerstone of financial accountability and transparency for small businesses. At its core, effective recordkeeping involves systematically gathering, organizing, and storing financial and operational information related to your business. The benefits of maintaining accurate and comprehensive records are multifaceted:

1. Financial Management and Planning

Accurate records provide a clear snapshot of your business's financial health. From revenue and expenses to cash flow patterns, these insights empower informed decision-making and strategic financial planning. Whether you're assessing profitability or planning for expansion, your records serve as a compass guiding your business through financial terrain.

2. Regulatory Compliance

Small businesses are subject to various local, state, and federal regulations. From tax obligations to industry-specific compliance requirements, maintaining meticulous records ensures that you can demonstrate adherence to these regulations. This not only safeguards your business from potential legal issues but also fosters a culture of transparency and responsibility.

3. Tax Preparation and Audits

Come tax season, comprehensive records streamline the tax preparation process. With organized financial records, you can more accurately report income, claim eligible deductions, and navigate the filing process efficiently. Additionally, in the event of an audit, having well-documented records is your best defense. It not only simplifies the audit process but also provides evidence of your business's financial integrity.

4. Operational Efficiency

Beyond financial matters, effective recordkeeping contributes to overall operational efficiency. From inventory management to customer interactions, keeping detailed records enables smoother day-to-day operations. This, in turn, enhances customer service, reduces errors, and fosters a proactive approach to problem-solving.

Essential Elements of Recordkeeping

To harness the full benefits of recordkeeping, small businesses should focus on capturing and organizing key pieces of information. The essential elements of effective recordkeeping include:

1. Income and Sales Records

Accurately documenting all sources of income is paramount. This includes sales receipts, invoices, and any other forms of revenue generated by your business. Tracking sales trends and customer behavior provides valuable insights into your business's financial performance.

2. Expense Records

Maintain detailed records of all business-related expenses. From office supplies to utility bills, every expenditure should be documented. Categorizing expenses facilitates budgeting and helps identify areas for potential cost savings.

3. Bank Statements and Financial Statements

Regularly reconcile your business's bank statements with your internal records. Financial statements, including balance sheets and income statements, offer a comprehensive overview of your business's financial position. These documents are invaluable for strategic decision-making and financial planning.

4. Tax Documents

Organize and retain all relevant tax documents, including W-2s, 1099s, and any correspondence with tax authorities. A well-maintained tax file ensures a smooth tax preparation process and simplifies audits or inquiries.

5. Employee Records

If your business has employees, maintain accurate records related to their employment. This includes payroll records, tax withholding forms, and any relevant employment agreements. Compliance with labor laws and regulations relies on thorough employee recordkeeping.

6. Contracts and Agreements

Keep copies of all contracts, agreements, and legal documents related to your business. This encompasses agreements with clients, vendors, landlords, and any other relevant parties. These records are critical for resolving disputes, ensuring compliance, and protecting your business's legal interests.

7. Inventory Records

For businesses involved in selling products, meticulous inventory records are essential. Track quantities, values, and movement of goods to optimize inventory management, prevent stockouts, and identify slow-moving items.

8. Communication Logs

Maintain records of all business-related communications. This includes emails, letters, and notes from meetings or phone calls. Thorough communication logs provide a historical record that can be invaluable in resolving disputes, tracking decisions, and understanding the evolution of business relationships.

Best Practices for Effective Recordkeeping

Establishing and maintaining effective recordkeeping practices requires a strategic and disciplined approach. Here are key best practices to guide your recordkeeping efforts:

1. Use Accounting Software

Investing in accounting software streamlines the recordkeeping process. These tools automate many aspects of financial tracking, reducing the likelihood of errors and facilitating real-time access to critical financial information.

2. Consistency is Key

Maintain consistency in how you document and categorize financial transactions. Consistency ensures accuracy and simplifies the retrieval of information when needed.

3. Regularly Reconcile Accounts

Regularly reconcile bank statements, financial statements, and other accounts to identify discrepancies promptly. This practice helps maintain the accuracy of your financial records.

4. Back Up Your Records

Implement robust backup procedures to protect against data loss. Regularly back up your financial records and store backups in a secure location, preferably offsite, to guard against unexpected events such as hardware failures or disasters.

5. Implement Access Controls

Limit access to financial records to only those individuals who require it for their roles. Implementing access controls helps safeguard sensitive financial information and reduces the risk of unauthorized changes.

6. Stay Current with Technology

Embrace technology advancements in recordkeeping, such as cloud-based solutions. Cloud storage not only provides secure data storage but also allows for remote access, facilitating collaboration and flexibility.

7. Educate and Train Staff

If you have employees involved in recordkeeping, provide training on the importance of accurate and consistent documentation. A well-informed team contributes to a culture of financial responsibility.

8. Regularly Review and Update Processes

As your business evolves, review and update your recordkeeping processes accordingly. Ensure that your systems and practices align with the changing needs and scale of your business.

Conclusion

Recordkeeping and documentation are not mere administrative tasks; they are indispensable tools for small business success. By treating recordkeeping as a strategic initiative, small businesses can unlock numerous benefits, from enhanced financial management to regulatory compliance and operational efficiency.

Self-Employment Taxes

For entrepreneurs venturing into the realm of self-employment, understanding and managing self-employment taxes is a critical aspect of financial responsibility. Unlike traditional employees who have taxes withheld by employers, self-employed individuals are responsible for handling their own tax obligations. In this comprehensive guide, we will explore the intricacies of self-employment taxes, examining what they entail, how they are calculated, and strategies for managing this financial responsibility.

Unraveling the Basics of Self-Employment Taxes

1. What Are Self-Employment Taxes?

Self-employment taxes represent the Social Security and Medicare taxes that individuals must pay when they work for themselves. While employees typically split these taxes with their employers, self-employed individuals are responsible for the full amount, often referred to as the self-employment tax.

2. Components of Self-Employment Taxes

Self-employment taxes consist of two main components:

- **Social Security Tax:** This tax funds the Social Security program and is calculated on a percentage of your net earnings. As of the last available information in 2022, the Social Security tax rate is 12.4%. However, only income up to a certain limit (known as the Social Security wage base) is subject to this tax.
- **Medicare Tax:** This tax supports the Medicare program and is levied on your entire net earnings. The Medicare tax rate is 2.9%. Additionally, if your income exceeds a certain threshold, you may be subject to an additional 0.9% Medicare tax.

Calculating Self-Employment Taxes

1. Determining Net Earnings

To calculate self-employment taxes, you first need to determine your net earnings from self-employment. This involves subtracting your deductible business expenses from your total business income.

2. Applying Social Security and Medicare Rates

Once you've established your net earnings, you apply the respective Social Security and Medicare tax rates to calculate the amounts owed. Keep in mind the Social Security wage base limit when determining the portion subject to the Social Security tax.

3. Completing IRS Schedule SE

Self-employed individuals use IRS Schedule SE to calculate and report their self-employment taxes. This form allows you to account for both the Social Security and Medicare taxes owed.

Strategies for Managing Self-Employment Taxes

1. Quarterly Estimated Tax Payments

Self-employed individuals are generally required to make quarterly estimated tax payments to cover their income tax and self-employment tax liabilities. Failure to do so may result in penalties. Calculating and paying estimated taxes helps distribute the financial responsibility throughout the year.

2. Keep Meticulous Records

Accurate recordkeeping is essential for determining your net earnings and identifying deductible business expenses. Maintain detailed records of your income, expenses, and receipts, ensuring that you can substantiate your figures in the event of an audit.

3. Explore Business Deductions

Maximizing business deductions can help lower your net earnings and, consequently, your self-employment tax liability. Common business deductions include expenses related to office space, equipment, supplies, and business-related travel.

4. Consider Retirement Contributions

Contributing to a retirement plan can have dual benefits. Not only does it help secure your financial future, but certain contributions may also be deductible, reducing your taxable income and, consequently, your self-employment tax liability.

5. Understand the Qualified Business Income Deduction (QBI)

The Qualified Business Income Deduction, introduced as part of the Tax Cuts and Jobs Act, provides eligible self-employed individuals with a deduction of up to 20% of their qualified business income. Understanding the nuances of this deduction can lead to significant tax savings.

6. Consult with a Tax Professional

Given the complexities of self-employment taxes, seeking guidance from a tax professional is a prudent step. Tax professionals can provide personalized advice, help identify additional deductions, and ensure compliance with ever-changing tax laws.

7. Plan for Additional Medicare Tax

If your income exceeds certain thresholds, you may be subject to an additional 0.9% Medicare tax on earnings above those thresholds. Understanding these thresholds and planning accordingly can prevent surprises at tax time.

8. Stay Informed about Tax Law Changes

Tax laws are subject to change, and staying informed about updates is crucial. Be aware of any modifications to self-employment tax rates, deduction limits, or other relevant regulations that may impact your financial obligations.

Conclusion

For self-employed individuals, mastering the intricacies of self-employment taxes is an essential component of financial management. While the responsibility may seem daunting, a proactive and informed approach can turn it into an opportunity for strategic tax planning and savings.

For self-employed individuals, the responsibility of managing taxes extends beyond the annual tax season. Quarterly estimated taxes become a crucial component of financial planning, ensuring that the IRS receives a steady stream of income throughout the year. In this guide, we'll explore the significance of quarterly estimated taxes, the process of calculating them, and essential strategies for staying on top of your tax obligations.

Understanding Quarterly Estimated Taxes

1. What are Quarterly Estimated Taxes?

Quarterly estimated taxes are payments made by self-employed individuals to cover their income tax and self-employment tax liabilities. Unlike traditional employees who have taxes withheld from their paychecks, self-employed individuals are responsible for making these estimated tax payments directly to the IRS.

2. Who Needs to Pay Quarterly Estimated Taxes?

If you expect to owe $1,000 or more in taxes when you file your annual return, you are generally required to make quarterly estimated tax payments. This includes self-employed individuals, freelancers, contractors, and anyone with substantial sources of income not subject to withholding.

Calculating and Paying Quarterly Estimated Taxes

1. Estimating Your Annual Income and Deductions

Begin by estimating your total annual income and identifying potential deductions. This includes business income, investment income, and any other sources of income. Deductible business expenses can help lower your taxable income.

2. Determining Your Tax Liability

Calculate your estimated annual tax liability by applying the appropriate tax rates to your taxable income. Consider both income tax and self-employment tax when determining the total amount owed.

3. Dividing the Annual Tax Liability

To determine the quarterly estimated tax payments, divide your estimated annual tax liability by four. This creates equal payments to be made each quarter, aligning with the IRS's quarterly payment schedule.

4. IRS Schedule C and Form 1040-ES

Use IRS Schedule C to report your business income and expenses. The resulting net profit or loss is then transferred to Form 1040-ES, where you calculate your estimated tax liability and determine the quarterly payments.

5. Payment Deadlines

Quarterly estimated tax payments are typically due on the 15th of April, June, September, and January of the following year. It's important to mark these dates on your calendar and plan accordingly to avoid penalties.

Strategies for Managing Quarterly Estimated Taxes

1. Stay Organized with Recordkeeping

Maintain meticulous records of your income and expenses throughout the year. This not only aids in accurate tax calculations but also provides a solid foundation for potential deductions.

2. Use Accounting Software

Leverage accounting software to streamline the tracking of your financial transactions. These tools can help automate calculations, reducing the likelihood of errors in your estimated tax calculations.

3. Adjusting Payments as Needed

If your income fluctuates or experiences significant changes, be prepared to adjust your quarterly estimated tax payments accordingly. Failing to do so can result in underpayment penalties or a large tax bill at year-end.

4. Take Advantage of Deductions and Credits

Explore available deductions and tax credits to reduce your taxable income. This can positively impact your estimated tax liability and result in lower quarterly payments.

5. Consult with a Tax Professional

If you find the process of calculating and managing quarterly estimated taxes challenging, consider seeking guidance from a tax professional. They can provide personalized advice based on your specific circumstances, helping you navigate the complexities with confidence.

6. Plan for Additional Tax Obligations

Be aware of any additional tax obligations that may arise, such as the Net Investment Income Tax or the Additional Medicare Tax. Understanding these obligations ensures accurate quarterly payments.

Conclusion

Managing quarterly estimated taxes is a fundamental aspect of financial responsibility for self-employed individuals. By understanding the process, staying organized, and implementing effective strategies, you can navigate this aspect of your financial obligations with confidence. Remember that the goal is not only to fulfill your tax responsibilities but also to optimize your financial position, contributing to the long-term success of your self-employed venture.

Small businesses play a pivotal role in driving economic growth, and the tax code recognizes their importance by offering various credits to support their development. Understanding and leveraging these tax credits is crucial for small business owners seeking to optimize their financial position. In this comprehensive guide, we will explore a variety of tax credits available to small businesses, shedding light on their eligibility criteria, potential benefits, and strategies for harnessing these opportunities.

1. Research and Development (R&D) Tax Credit

What is it?

The Research and Development (R&D) Tax Credit is designed to encourage innovation by providing tax incentives to businesses engaged in qualifying research activities. While often associated with large corporations, small businesses can also benefit from this credit.

Eligibility Criteria:

To qualify, a business must engage in activities that meet certain criteria, such as:

- Conducting research to develop a new or improved product, process, or software.
- Facing uncertainty about the feasibility or methodology of the research.
- Incurring expenses related to wages, supplies, or contract research.

Potential Benefits:

The R&D Tax Credit can result in a dollar-for-dollar reduction in income tax liability, making it a valuable incentive for small businesses investing in research and development.

2. Small Business Health Care Tax Credit

What is it?

The Small Business Health Care Tax Credit is aimed at assisting small businesses that offer health insurance coverage to their employees. It helps alleviate the financial burden of providing health care benefits.

Eligibility Criteria:

To qualify, a small business must:

- Have fewer than 25 full-time equivalent employees.
- Pay average annual wages that fall below a specified threshold.
- Contribute at least 50% of employees' self-only health insurance premiums.

Potential Benefits:

The credit can be as much as 50% of the employer's contribution to employee health coverage premiums, making it an impactful incentive for businesses prioritizing employee well-being.

3. Work Opportunity Tax Credit (WOTC)

What is it?

The Work Opportunity Tax Credit (WOTC) encourages businesses to hire individuals from specific target groups facing barriers to employment, such as veterans, ex-felons, and individuals receiving certain government assistance.

Eligibility Criteria:

Employers may be eligible for the WOTC when hiring individuals from designated target groups and meeting certain criteria related to employment duration and hours worked.

Potential Benefits:

The WOTC provides a tax credit ranging from $1,200 to $9,600 per qualified employee, offering a financial incentive for businesses to diversify their workforce and support individuals facing employment challenges.

4. Employee Retention Credit (ERC)

What is it?

The Employee Retention Credit (ERC) was introduced as part of COVID-19 relief efforts and is designed to support businesses that retained employees during challenging economic times.

Eligibility Criteria:

Eligibility criteria for the ERC include experiencing a significant decline in gross receipts or facing government-imposed restrictions due to the pandemic.

Potential Benefits:

The ERC offers a refundable tax credit of up to $5,000 per employee for wages paid between March 13, 2020, and December 31, 2021. The credit aims to provide financial relief to businesses navigating the economic impact of the pandemic.

5. Section 179 Deduction

What is it?

While not a traditional tax credit, the Section 179 Deduction allows businesses to deduct the cost of qualifying property as an expense rather than depreciating it over time. It can significantly reduce taxable income.

Eligibility Criteria:

Businesses must meet specific criteria related to the type and cost of property being deducted. Common eligible items include equipment, machinery, and certain vehicles.

Potential Benefits:

The Section 179 Deduction allows businesses to deduct the full cost of qualifying property, up to specified limits. For small businesses, this can result in immediate tax savings, promoting investment in essential assets.

6. Energy-Efficient Commercial Buildings Deduction

What is it?

The Energy-Efficient Commercial Buildings Deduction, also known as the Section 179D deduction, encourages businesses to invest in energy-efficient building improvements.

Eligibility Criteria:

Eligible businesses include those that make energy-efficient improvements to commercial buildings, such as lighting, HVAC, and building envelope upgrades.

Potential Benefits:

The deduction allows businesses to deduct up to $1.80 per square foot for qualifying energy-efficient improvements. This not only supports environmental sustainability but also provides tax savings for eligible businesses.

Strategies for Optimizing Tax Credits

1. Stay Informed about Changes

Tax laws and regulations evolve, and staying informed is crucial. Regularly check for updates and changes to ensure you are aware of the latest opportunities and requirements.

2. Consult with Tax Professionals

Engaging with tax professionals can provide valuable insights tailored to your specific business circumstances. They can help identify eligible credits, ensure compliance, and optimize your overall tax strategy.

3. Maintain Accurate Records

Accurate recordkeeping is essential for claiming tax credits. Keep detailed records of relevant expenses, employee information, and any other documentation required to support your claims.

4. Plan Strategically

Strategic planning involves aligning your business activities with available tax credits. Consider how certain investments or hiring decisions may qualify for credits, and incorporate this knowledge into your overall business strategy.

5. Leverage Multiple Credits

Explore opportunities to combine multiple tax credits. For example, a business may qualify for both the R&D Tax Credit and the Small Business Health Care Tax Credit, enhancing overall tax benefits.

Conclusion

Tax credits present valuable opportunities for small businesses to optimize their financial position, invest strategically, and support their workforce. By understanding the eligibility criteria, potential benefits, and implementing strategic approaches, small business owners can navigate the complex landscape of tax credits with confidence. Remember that each business is unique, and consulting with tax professionals can provide tailored guidance, ensuring that you maximize available opportunities and contribute to the long-term success of your enterprise.

Common Tax Mistakes to Avoid

In the intricate world of small business finances, navigating the tax landscape can be both challenging and critical to success. Small business owners often find themselves juggling multiple responsibilities, and mistakes in tax matters can lead to financial setbacks and regulatory issues. In this comprehensive guide, we will explore common tax mistakes that small businesses should avoid, shedding light on strategies to stay compliant and optimize their financial position.

1. Inadequate Recordkeeping

The Mistake:

Inaccurate or incomplete recordkeeping can lead to a cascade of tax-related problems. Without meticulous records, businesses may struggle to substantiate income, deductions, and compliance with tax regulations.

The Solution:

Implement robust recordkeeping practices. Use accounting software to track income and expenses, retain receipts and invoices, and maintain organized records. Accurate recordkeeping not only ensures compliance but also facilitates strategic financial planning.

2. Misclassifying Workers

The Mistake:

Misclassifying workers as independent contractors instead of employees, or vice versa, can result in tax liabilities and legal issues. Each classification has distinct tax implications, and misclassification can lead to penalties and fines.

The Solution:

Understand the criteria that distinguish employees from independent contractors. Factors such as control, financial arrangements, and the nature of the work relationship play a role. If in doubt, seek legal advice to ensure proper worker classification.

3. Neglecting Quarterly Estimated Taxes

The Mistake:

Failing to make quarterly estimated tax payments can lead to underpayment penalties. Self-employed individuals and businesses with substantial income not subject to withholding should make these payments to cover their tax liabilities throughout the year.

The Solution:

Stay organized and estimate your tax liability accurately. Make quarterly estimated tax payments to avoid penalties and spread the financial responsibility throughout the year. Regularly review and adjust payments based on changes in income.

4. Overlooking Deductible Expenses

The Mistake:

Failure to take advantage of eligible deductions means businesses pay more in taxes than necessary. Overlooking deductible expenses, such as business-related travel, equipment purchases, or home office expenses, can result in missed opportunities for tax savings.

The Solution:

Stay informed about eligible deductions for your industry and business structure. Keep detailed records of expenses and work with tax professionals to identify all potential deductions. Properly documenting and claiming deductions can significantly reduce taxable income.

5. Ignoring Tax Deadlines

The Mistake:

Missing tax deadlines can result in penalties and interest charges. Whether it's filing income tax returns, making quarterly estimated tax payments, or providing necessary documentation, adherence to deadlines is crucial.

The Solution:

Create a comprehensive tax calendar that includes all relevant deadlines. Set reminders and allocate sufficient time to gather necessary information. Meeting deadlines not only avoids penalties but also ensures a smoother tax filing process.

6. Failing to Maximize Tax Credits

The Mistake:

Overlooking available tax credits means missing out on opportunities for significant tax savings. Small businesses may qualify for various credits, such as the Research and Development Tax Credit or the Small Business Health Care Tax Credit.

The Solution:

Stay informed about available tax credits for small businesses. Understand the eligibility criteria and requirements for each credit. Strategically plan business activities to align with qualifying criteria and leverage multiple credits whenever possible.

7. Disregarding Retirement Contributions

The Mistake:

Failing to contribute to retirement plans not only impacts employees' financial well-being but also means missing out on potential tax benefits. Contributions to certain retirement plans may be deductible, reducing taxable income.

The Solution:

Explore retirement plan options available to small businesses, such as Simplified Employee Pension (SEP) IRAs or 401(k) plans. Encourage employee participation and consider employer contributions.

Taking advantage of retirement-related tax benefits contributes to both financial security and tax savings.

8. Neglecting State and Local Taxes

The Mistake:

Focusing solely on federal taxes and overlooking state and local tax obligations can lead to compliance issues. Each jurisdiction has its own tax regulations, and failure to comply can result in penalties.

The Solution:

Understand the state and local tax requirements applicable to your business. Keep abreast of changes in tax laws at all levels of government. Consider enlisting the services of tax professionals with expertise in local tax regulations.

9. Not Seeking Professional Guidance

The Mistake:

Attempting to navigate complex tax matters without professional guidance can result in errors, oversights, and missed opportunities. Tax laws are intricate and subject to change, and professional expertise is invaluable in ensuring compliance and maximizing benefits.

The Solution:

Consult with tax professionals who specialize in small business taxation. Their expertise can help you navigate the complexities of the tax code, identify opportunities for savings, and ensure accurate and compliant tax filings.

Conclusion

Avoiding common tax mistakes is crucial for small businesses striving for financial health and compliance. By prioritizing accurate recordkeeping, understanding tax obligations, and seeking professional guidance, small business owners can navigate the tax landscape with confidence. Proactive tax planning, adherence to deadlines, and a commitment to staying informed about tax laws contribute to long-term financial success. Remember that each business is unique, and seeking personalized advice from tax professionals tailored to your specific circumstances is an investment in the financial resilience and growth of your enterprise.

Filing and Submission Process

The process of filing taxes is a pivotal aspect of financial management for small businesses. Navigating the complex landscape of tax regulations, deadlines, and documentation requires a strategic and systematic approach. In this comprehensive guide, we will delve into the intricacies of the filing and submission process, providing small business owners with insights into key considerations, best practices, and strategies for a smooth and compliant tax filing experience.

Understanding the Basics

1. Business Structure and Tax Forms

The first step in the filing process is understanding the tax forms applicable to your business structure. Different structures, such as sole proprietorships, partnerships, corporations, and LLCs, have distinct tax requirements. Familiarize yourself with the relevant IRS forms, including:

- **Sole Proprietorship:** Use Schedule C (Form 1040).
- **Partnership:** File Form 1065.

- **Corporation:** File either Form 1120 (C Corporation) or Form 1120-S (S Corporation).
- **Limited Liability Company (LLC):** Depending on the election, LLCs may file as sole proprietorships, partnerships, or corporations.

2. Gather Necessary Documentation

Collecting and organizing the required documentation is a critical aspect of the filing process. This includes:

- **Income Documents:** Gather records of all sources of income, including sales, services, and any other business-related income.
- **Expense Receipts:** Keep detailed receipts for all business-related expenses. This includes invoices, receipts for purchases, and documentation for deductible expenses.
- **Bank Statements:** Reconcile bank statements to ensure accuracy in reporting income and expenses.
- **Employee Information:** If applicable, have records of employee wages, tax withholdings, and any other relevant employment information.
- **Financial Statements:** Prepare financial statements, including balance sheets and

income statements, to provide a comprehensive overview of your business's financial health.

Best Practices for a Smooth Filing Process

1. Stay Organized Throughout the Year

Rather than scrambling to gather documents at tax time, maintain organized records throughout the year. Implement a robust recordkeeping system to track income, expenses, and other financial transactions.

2. Adhere to Deadlines

Familiarize yourself with tax deadlines to avoid late filing penalties. Key deadlines include:

- **Individual Income Tax Return (Form 1040):** Generally due on April 15th.
- **Partnership Tax Return (Form 1065):** Due on March 15th.
- **Corporate Tax Return (Form 1120):** Due on April 15th (for calendar year corporations).

3. Consider E-Filing

Electronic filing (e-filing) offers numerous advantages, including faster processing, reduced errors, and confirmation of receipt. Many tax preparation software options facilitate e-filing for various forms.

4. Review Tax Law Changes

Tax laws can undergo changes, impacting deductions, credits, and filing requirements. Stay informed about any modifications that may affect your business, and adjust your filing strategy accordingly.

Steps in the Filing Process

1. Complete Relevant Tax Forms

Start by completing the appropriate tax forms based on your business structure. Provide accurate and detailed information, ensuring that all applicable sections are filled out correctly.

2. Calculate Tax Liability

Once the forms are completed, calculate your tax liability. Consider deductions, credits, and any other factors that may affect the final amount owed or refunded.

3. Review and Verify Information

Thoroughly review all the information on your tax forms before submission. Check for accuracy in names, addresses, and numerical figures. A comprehensive review reduces the likelihood of errors.

4. Choose a Filing Method

Decide whether to file by mail or electronically. E-filing is generally faster and more convenient, but some businesses may opt for traditional paper filing.

5. Submit the Forms

If filing by mail, send the completed forms to the designated IRS address. If e-filing, follow the instructions provided by your chosen tax preparation software or service.

6. Payment of Taxes Owed

If you owe taxes, ensure timely payment. Options include mailing a check with your paper return or using electronic payment methods if filing electronically.

7. Retain Copies of Filed Documents

Keep copies of all filed tax documents, including the completed forms and any supporting documentation.

These records are essential for future reference and in case of audits.

Common Pitfalls to Avoid

1. Incomplete or Inaccurate Information

Providing incomplete or inaccurate information on tax forms can lead to delays, penalties, or audits. Take the time to ensure all information is accurate and up-to-date.

2. Missing Deductions or Credits

Failing to claim eligible deductions or credits means missing out on potential tax savings. Stay informed about available incentives and ensure you take advantage of all applicable opportunities.

3. Ignoring State and Local Taxes

In addition to federal taxes, businesses must comply with state and local tax obligations. Ignoring these requirements can result in penalties and legal issues.

4. Neglecting Quarterly Estimated Taxes

If your business is required to make quarterly estimated tax payments, neglecting these obligations can lead to underpayment penalties. Stay organized and make timely payments throughout the year.

5. Misclassifying Workers

Properly classify workers as employees or independent contractors. Misclassification can result in tax liabilities and legal consequences.

Strategies for Optimizing the Filing Process

1. Leverage Technology

Explore tax preparation software and other digital tools to streamline the filing process. These tools often automate calculations, reducing the risk of errors.

2. Consult with Tax Professionals

If the filing process is complex or you encounter challenges, consider consulting with tax professionals. Their expertise can help you navigate intricacies and ensure compliance.

3. Plan for the Future

Use the filing process as an opportunity to assess your business's financial health. Identify areas for improvement, plan for future tax obligations, and implement strategies for increased efficiency.

4. Invest in Education

Stay educated about tax laws and regulations that pertain to your business. Attend workshops, webinars, or seek guidance from tax professionals to enhance your understanding.

5. Establish a Recordkeeping System

Maintain a robust recordkeeping system throughout the year. Invest in accounting software and organizational practices that facilitate accurate and efficient record management.

Conclusion

The filing and submission process is a crucial aspect of small business financial management. By understanding the basics, adopting best practices, and avoiding common pitfalls, business owners can navigate the complexities of tax filing with confidence. Staying organized, adhering to deadlines, and leveraging available technologies contribute to a smoother and more efficient filing experience.

Remember that each business is unique, and seeking personalized advice from tax professionals tailored to your specific circumstances is an investment in the financial resilience and growth of your enterprise. Approach the filing process strategically, view it as an opportunity for financial assessment and planning, and position your business for continued success in the dynamic landscape of tax compliance.

State and Local Tax Considerations

Small businesses operate within a complex web of tax obligations that extend beyond federal requirements. State and local taxes add an additional layer of complexity, as each jurisdiction may have its own regulations, rates, and compliance standards. In this comprehensive guide, we will explore the various aspects of state and local tax considerations for small businesses, providing insights into key considerations, common challenges, and strategies for navigating this intricate landscape.

Understanding State and Local Taxes

1. Types of State and Local Taxes

State and local taxes can take various forms, and the specific taxes applicable to a business depend on its location. Common types of state and local taxes include:

- **Sales Tax:** Imposed on the sale of tangible goods and, in some cases, certain services.
- **Income Tax:** Imposed on business profits at the state level. States may also levy income taxes on individual business owners.

- **Property Tax:** Levied on real property owned by businesses, such as land and buildings.
- **Business License Taxes:** Some jurisdictions require businesses to obtain and pay for a business license to operate within their boundaries.
- **Payroll Taxes:** Certain localities impose taxes on employee wages.

2. Nexus and Multi-State Operations

Determining a business's nexus, or its connection to a particular jurisdiction, is crucial for understanding state and local tax obligations. If a business operates in multiple states, it may be subject to taxes in each jurisdiction where it has a significant presence or conducts business activities. Establishing nexus typically involves factors such as physical presence, sales volume, or the number of transactions within a jurisdiction.

Key Considerations for Small Businesses

1. Registration and Compliance

Small businesses must be aware of their registration requirements in each jurisdiction where they operate.

This includes registering for sales tax permits, obtaining business licenses, and complying with state and local regulations. Failing to register appropriately can result in penalties and legal consequences.

2. Sales Tax Collection and Reporting

For businesses involved in the sale of goods or certain services, understanding and complying with sales tax requirements is crucial. This involves collecting sales tax from customers, remitting it to the appropriate taxing authorities, and regularly reporting sales tax information. Compliance with changing sales tax rates and rules can be challenging but is essential for avoiding penalties.

3. State Income Tax Filings

Businesses operating in states with income taxes must file state income tax returns in addition to federal returns. The calculation of state taxable income may differ from federal taxable income, and businesses need to understand state-specific rules for deductions, credits, and apportionment.

4. Property Tax Assessments

Property tax obligations can significantly impact businesses that own real property. Businesses should be aware of how property is assessed, the applicable tax rates, and any available exemptions or abatements. Regularly reviewing property tax assessments ensures accurate billing and the identification of potential savings opportunities.

5. Employee Withholding and Payroll Taxes

Complying with state and local payroll tax obligations is essential for businesses with employees. This includes understanding state income tax withholding requirements, unemployment insurance taxes, and any other local payroll taxes. Failing to withhold and remit these taxes can lead to penalties and legal issues.

6. Local Business Taxes and Fees

Certain localities impose specific business taxes or fees. This may include gross receipts taxes, payroll taxes, or fees for specific business activities. Small businesses need to be aware of these local requirements and factor them into their overall tax planning.

Common Challenges and Pitfalls

1. Changing Regulations

State and local tax regulations can change frequently, and businesses must stay informed about updates that may impact their tax obligations. Failing to adapt to regulatory changes can lead to compliance issues and potential penalties.

2. Nexus Determination

The concept of nexus is complex, and businesses may struggle to accurately determine their connection to various jurisdictions. This challenge is particularly relevant for businesses engaged in e-commerce or those with multi-state operations.

3. Sales Tax Compliance for Online Sales

E-commerce businesses face challenges related to sales tax compliance, especially with the growth of online sales. Determining when and where to collect sales tax for online transactions requires a nuanced understanding of state and local rules.

4. Recordkeeping Challenges

Managing records for multiple jurisdictions can be overwhelming. Businesses must establish effective recordkeeping systems to track sales, expenses, and other relevant information specific to each state or locality where they operate.

5. Navigating Multiple Tax Authorities

Operating in multiple states means dealing with multiple tax authorities, each with its own requirements and procedures. This complexity can pose administrative challenges for small businesses with limited resources.

Strategies for Navigating State and Local Taxes

1. Consult with Tax Professionals

Given the complexity of state and local tax considerations, consulting with tax professionals is highly advisable. Tax experts can help businesses understand their obligations, navigate changing regulations, and optimize their tax positions.

2. Invest in Technology

Utilize tax software and technology solutions to automate certain aspects of tax compliance. This includes sales tax calculations, recordkeeping, and payroll processing. Technology can help businesses stay organized and reduce the risk of errors.

3. Conduct Regular Nexus Reviews

Regularly review business activities and assess whether they establish nexus in new jurisdictions. This proactive approach helps businesses stay ahead of compliance requirements and avoid surprises.

4. Stay Informed about Changes

Monitor state and local tax law changes that may impact your business. Subscribe to updates from tax authorities, attend relevant workshops or webinars, and engage with industry associations to stay informed about evolving regulations.

5. Centralize Tax Compliance Management

Centralizing the management of state and local tax compliance can enhance efficiency. Implement a system that allows for centralized recordkeeping, reporting, and coordination with tax professionals.

6. Engage in Strategic Planning

Strategic tax planning involves evaluating the overall tax impact of business decisions. Consider the tax implications when expanding operations, making significant purchases, or engaging in other activities that may affect state and local tax obligations.

Conclusion

State and local tax considerations add a layer of complexity to the financial landscape for small businesses. Navigating this intricate terrain requires a combination of awareness, strategic planning, and compliance diligence. By understanding the types of state and local taxes, staying informed about key considerations, and adopting proactive strategies, small businesses can optimize their tax positions and avoid common pitfalls.

www.ingramcontent.com/pod-product-compliance
Lightning Source LLC
Chambersburg PA
CBHW062251290526
45794CB00006B/2498